LM 0922105 0

KT-514-869

Lambeth
Libraries

08/06

SOUTH LAMBETH LIBRARY
CHILDRENS SERVICES
180 SOUTH LAMBETH ROAD
SW8 1QP
TEL: 020 7926 0705

Items must be returned
on or before the last date
stamped below, or
overdue charges will be
made.

Renewals may be made
by personal application,
by post, or by telephone.

0 8 APR 2006

- 3 1 4 DEC 2006
JAN 2007
9/10
1 3 SEP 2010

ES150 8812A AR (5.02)

LAMBETH LIBRARIES	
0922105 0	
PETERS	781.64
07-Feb-05	£11.50
C	

STAR FILES

Justin Timberlake

Dan Whitcombe

www.raintreepublishers.co.uk

Visit our website to find out more information about **Raintree** books.

To order:
 Phone 44 (0) 1865 888113
 Send a fax to 44 (0) 1865 314091
Visit the Raintree Bookshop at **www.raintreepublishers.co.uk** to browse our catalogue and order online.

Produced for Raintree by
White-Thomson Publishing Ltd
Bridgewater Business Centre
210 High Street, Lewes BN7 2NH

First published in Great Britain by Raintree,
Halley Court, Jordan Hill, Oxford OX2 8EJ,
part of Harcourt Education.
Raintree is a registered trademark of Harcourt
Education Ltd.

© Harcourt Education Ltd 2005
The moral right of the proprietor has
been asserted.

All rights reserved. No part of this publication
may be reproduced, stored in a retrieval system,
or transmitted in any form or by any means,
electronic, mechanical, photocopying, recording
or otherwise, without either the prior written
permission of the publishers or a licence permitting
restricted copying in the United Kingdom issued by
the Copyright Licensing Agency Ltd, 90 Tottenham
Court Road, London W1T 4LP (www.cla.co.uk).

Editorial: Nick Hunter and Catherine Clarke
Design: Leishman Design and Michelle Lisseter
Picture Research: Nicola Hodgson
Production: Kevin Blackman
Project Management: Nicola Hodgson

Originated by Dot Gradations Ltd
Printed and bound in China by South China
Printing Company

ISBN 1 844 43833 3
09 08 07 06 05
10 9 8 7 6 5 4 3 2 1

**British Library Cataloguing in
Publication Data**
Whitcombe, Dan
Justin Timberlake. – (Star Files)
782.4' 2166' 092
A full catalogue record for this book is
available from the British Library.

Acknowledgements
The publishers would like to thank the
following for permission to reproduce
photographs: Corbis pp. **16**, **26** (r); Getty
Images pp. **6** (t), **15** (t), **25**, **30**, **32** (r); Retna
Pictures pp. **7** (t), **8–9**, **11** (l), **14**, **15** (b), **20**,
21 (t), **23** (t), **23** (b), **31** (r), **37**, **40** (l), **42**,
43 (r); Rex Features pp. **4**, **6** (b), **7** (b), **8**, **9**,
10, **11** (r), **12**, **13** (l), **13** (r), **17** (t), **17** (b),
18, **19** (l), **19** (r), **21** (b), **22** (l), **22** (r), **24** (l),
24 (r), **26** (l), **27** (l), **27** (r), **28**, **29** (l), **29** (r),
31 (l), **32** (l), **33**, **34**, **35** (l), **35** (r), **36**, **38**,
39 (l), **39** (r), **40**, **41**, **43** (l). Cover photograph
reproduced with permission of Retna Pictures.

Quote sources p. **4** The *Observer Magazine*:
6 October 2002; p. **11** *USA Today*, 20 July
1999; p. **12** *Justin Timberlake: The Unofficial
Book*, Martin Roach; p. **20** MTV interview,
September 2002; p. **23** interview with
groovevolt.com; p. **25** MTV interview,
September 2002; p. **28** *Vibe* magazine,
February 2003; p. **33** The *Guardian,* January
2003; p. **41** The *Herald* 25 January 2003;
p. **42** VH1 interview, 18 November 2002;
The *Guardian*, 31 January 2003.

The publishers would like to thank Voirrey
Carr and Simone Apel for their assistance in
the preparation of this book.

Every effort has been made to contact
copyright holders of any material reproduced
in this book. Any omissions will be rectified
in subsequent printings if notice is given to
the publishers.

The paper used to print this book comes from
sustainable resources.

Disclaimer: This book is not authorized or
approved by Justin Timberlake.

Contents

Justin crazy 4

Starting out 6

Lives in sync 12

Going solo 18

Style and image 26

Personal interests 30

Media spotlight 34

Now and then 42

Find out more 44

Glossary 46

Index 48

Any words appearing in the text in bold, **like this**, are explained in the Glossary. You can also look out for them in the Star words box at the bottom of each page.

Justin crazy

ALL ABOUT JUSTIN

Full name: Justin Randall Timberlake
Born: 6.30pm, 31 January 1981
Place of birth: St Jude's Medical Center, Memphis, Tennessee
Family: Randy (father); Lynn (mother); Paul Harless (stepfather); Lisa (stepmother); Jonathan and Stephen (half-brothers)
Height: 6' 1" (1.86 metres) **Eyes:** Blue
Hair: Sandy blond **Star sign:** Aquarius
Hobbies: Computer games, golf, basketball
Favourite musicians: Stevie Wonder, Michael Jackson, Marvin Gaye
Sporting hero: The basketball player Michael Jordan
First hit: 'I want you back' with 'NSYNC
Other Interests: The Justin Timberlake Foundation, a music charity in Memphis

Justin Timberlake is one of the hottest properties in the pop world. He is very successful. Getting to the top was not easy, though. Justin has had to work hard for his breaks. Justin's career started when he was spotted on a television talent show. He was just eleven years old.

Music star

Justin has been a children's television presenter. He has been the lead singer in a very popular boy band. He has also been half of one of the biggest celebrity couples in the pop world. Now he has the world at his feet. What about the future?

⭐ Star fact

Justin's curly hair became his **trademark** when he was younger. Not everyone liked it, though. Justin admits that one of his nicknames was 'brillo pad'!

Star words   trademark something that is typical about a person

Justin could continue to become a great pop star. He could turn to music **production**. He may try becoming a film star. With his talent and dedication, not even Justin knows what the future holds.

> My boy is just what he is. He's got music. (Pharrell Williams of the Neptunes)

Find out later

How old was Justin when 'NSYNC formed?

Who came up with the name of 'NSYNC and what does it stand for?

Which famous hip-hop **producer** has Justin worked with?

Justin entertained thousands of fans at London's Wembley Arena in 2003.

production arranging and mixing the music when recording a song

Justin was born in Memphis, Tennessee, in 1981. Music was part of his life from the beginning. Justin's mother, Lynn, played several instruments when she was young, and her father had been a bass player. Justin's father, Randy, was a famous **bluegrass** singer.

Home life

Justin's family lived in a nice **suburb** of Memphis. His early life was not all easy, though. His parents separated when he was just two years old. Lynn remarried when Justin was four. Her new husband was a banker called Paul Harless.

Justin and the rest of 'NSYNC show off their pets.

Justin's dogs

Two of the best reasons for Justin to spend time at his mother's house are the two family Yorkshire Terrier dogs. Their names are Bearlie and Bella, and they are both fans of Justin.

Memphis is famous for its blues musicians.

Star words bluegrass mixture of country music and blues that is common in the southern and midwest states of the USA

Paul is the man that Justin thought of as his father when he was growing up. Randy also married again and had two more sons. These are Justin's half-brothers, Jonathan and Stephen.

★ ★ ★ ★ ★ ★ ★ ★ ★ ★

Memphis stars

Justin was not the first great musician to come out of Memphis, Tennessee. Other **icons** include the rock 'n' roll legend Jerry Lee Lewis. He had a massive hit with the song 'Great balls of fire' in the 1950s. Memphis's most famous musician is 'The King': Elvis Presley.

★ ★ ★ ★ ★ ★ ★ ★ ★ ★

Like Justin, Elvis Presley came from Memphis.

★ Star fact

MTV was launched in 1981. So Justin and one of the most famous television channels dedicated to music were born in the same year!

Justin and his future manager-mum.

icon important or famous person that you look up to and try to be like

Singing always felt natural for Justin. As a child Justin sang at the services in the family's local Baptist church. At the age of eight he started singing lessons with a voice coach called Bob Westbrook. Justin and some of his friends even performed in a New Kids on the Block **tribute band** at school. Justin caused quite a stir with the girls at the concert. This was a taste of things to come!

Trying out
Justin wanted to be famous outside Memphis, however. From the age of nine he went on every talent show he could. One of his early performances was on the Grand Ole Opry show. This was a famous country music show in Tennessee.

First chance
When he was eleven, Justin got his biggest chance yet. A US television talent show called *Star Search* came to Memphis.

★ ★ ★ ★ ★ ★ ★ ★ ★ ★

Soul man
At his audition to join the television show the *Mickey Mouse Club*, Justin sang the classic soul hit, 'When a man loves a woman', by Percy Sledge (above).

★ ★ ★ ★ ★ ★ ★ ★ ★ ★

At the *Mickey Mouse Club*, Justin (in the middle) joined other talented kids including Britney Spears (in the centre of the front row).

Star words   tribute band musical group that plays another band's songs in a very similar style

Justin was chosen to appear on the show. He and his mother Lynn travelled to Orlando, Florida, to record the programme. This was Justin's first television appearance. In the programme he sang a country and western song, dressed in a cowboy suit. He did not win the competition, but he did get spotted by a **casting director**. The casting director was looking for children to appear on a television programme called the *Mickey Mouse Club* (also called *MMC*). Justin was invited to **audition** for the new series of the Disney programme.

★ ★ ★ ★ ★ ★ ★ ★ ★ ★ ★ ★

New Kids on the Block

New Kids on the Block (below) was the most famous boy band in the world in 1992. There was a lot of competition to be the 'next big thing'. Every audition saw kids queuing round the block for a chance. At the *MMC* auditions, Justin was one of just seven kids they picked for the show out of 2600 who tried out.

★ ★ ★ ★ ★ ★ ★ ★ ★ ★ ★ ★

casting director person who picks out new talent to appear on television or in films

Mickey Mouse Club

Justin joined Disney's *Mickey Mouse Club* in 1993. The show was in its sixth series. Some of the other '**Mouseketeers**' were already **veterans** of television. The main presenter, JC (Joshua Scott Chasez), was only seventeen years old, but he was an experienced professional.

The show

MMC was a remake of a US show from the 1950s. It was different from other pop music programmes because kids ran the show. It had stories, interviews, competitions, phone-ins and pop news. It also featured the latest chart hits. The kid presenters did everything. They even performed **cover versions** of the latest hits live on the show. They had to look the part, dance the steps and have great voices, too.

Melissa Joan Hart showed that being a Mouseketeer could lead the way to solo stardom.

A day's work

Being on the *Mickey Mouse Club* might sound fun and glamorous, but it was also very hard work. The kids working with JC had to catch the school bus at 7 a.m. each morning. They then spent the morning in class with a special tutor at Disney's MGM studio. They spent the afternoon rehearsing and 'doing wardrobe' to make the stars look just right for the occasion. This included clothes, hairstyle and make-up – for the boys as well as the girls. Finally they performed the three-hour show in front of a live audience in the evening. This was a bit more than your average school day!

★ ★ ★ ★ ★ ★ ★ ★ ★ ★

Teenage star

Melissa Joan Hart, better known as *Sabrina the Teenage Witch*, appeared in the early series of the *Mickey Mouse Club*.

★ ★ ★ ★ ★ ★ ★ ★ ★ ★

Star words   veteran someone with a lot of experience in something

The *MMC* kids: that's Britney Spears sitting on the floor, Christina Aguilera on the right and Justin at the back on the right.

Pop queens

Other young stars who appeared on the *MMC* included Britney Spears and Christina Aguilera (below). They are now two of the biggest female pop stars in the world. Christina once said: 'We used to joke around backstage and say "Whenever the show ends, we'll all go our separate ways and become stars."'

cover version recording or performance of a song by a different performer from the original

Lives in sync

★ ★ ★ ★ ★ ★ ★ ★ ★ ★

Showbiz pressure

Justin was only fourteen years old when 'NSYNC was formed. Sometimes the pressures of show business were hard for him to handle. Justin says: 'One day I broke down. I was crying and crying and I didn't know why.'

★ ★ ★ ★ ★ ★ ★ ★ ★ ★

Justin when he was fourteen.

The last series of the *Mickey Mouse Club* was in 1995, when Justin was fourteen. That left all of the **Mouseketeers** out of a job. Music had got Justin his part in the show. He was now a television star, but music was his first love. When the *MMC* came to an end, it was the perfect time for Justin to return to what he knew best.

JC and friends

While he was on the *MMC*, Justin became good friends with Joshua Chasez. JC had plans to form a boy band. Boy bands like the Backstreet Boys were very popular. Both Justin and JC had made contacts in the music business. They had the help of people like the **choreographer** Wade J Robson and the **producer** Pete Wylie. They started to try to make it in the music business.

Forming the band

Justin and JC moved back to Memphis from Florida, where the *MMC* had been filmed. They started looking for people to form a band with. They met up with Chris Kirkpatrick, who wanted to start a band with his friend, Joey Fatone. The four boys decided to try working together. Joey had a friend who was also interested in joining. The original fifth member was called Jason. He left after a short time. Justin then asked his old vocal coach, Bob Westbrook, if he knew anyone who might want to join.

Star words

choreographer person who makes up dance routines for pop videos and live performances

Bob put them in touch with Lance 'Lansten' Bass. The boys decided on a name, 'NSYNC, and the band was complete!

The Backstreet Boys were huge in 1995, and 'NSYNC wanted the same sort of success.

★ ★ ★ ★ ★ ★ ★ ★ ★ ★ ★ ★

Young stars

The New Kids on the Block had been huge in the early 1990s. By the mid-1990s the Backstreet Boys were the fastest-selling boy band of all time. Pop music had had young stars before then, though. Two of Justin's biggest musical heroes are Michael Jackson and Stevie Wonder (above). They had both been child stars.

★ ★ ★ ★ ★ ★ ★ ★ ★

Hard work

Being a pop star might sound like fun, but it was hard work too. 'NYSNC started out doing hundreds of **gigs** in schools, shopping centres and tiny venues across Europe and Asia before returning to the USA to **promote** their first album. Recording in the studio could be long and boring. The video for 'Tearin' up my heart' took 24 hours to film.

Five stars appeal

When Justin was not at school he was rehearsing in a warehouse with the other 'NSYNC boys. They recorded and sent out a video **demo**. To their delight, in 1996 they were taken on by Lou Pearlman and music manager Johnny Wright. Lou Pearlman was known in the music industry as 'Big Poppa'. These two men were behind the success of the Backstreet Boys.

Early days

From the summer of 1996 until the end of 1997, the band toured Europe, Africa, Asia and Latin America. They also recorded their first album, 'NSYNC.

★ Star fact

Coming up with a name was one of the band's hardest decisions. It was Justin's mother, Lynn, who came up with the idea of taking the last letter of each of their names: Justin, Chris, Joey, Jason (Lansten) and JC.

Justin and the rest of the band often earned as many headlines for their dress sense as for their music!

It was not until the beginning of 1998 that they tried to get into the US charts. They released the single, 'I want you back', in the USA in March 1998. From that moment on their lives would never be the same.

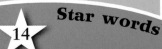

a cappella music in which no instruments, just singing voices, are used

BAND BIOS

Joshua Scott Chasez (JC)
Born: 8 August 1976, Washington, D.C.
Fun fact: JC's first teenage crush was on Carrie Fisher. She played Princess Leia in the original *Star Wars* films.

Christopher (Chris) Kirkpatrick
Born: 17 October 1971, Clarion, Pennsylvania
Fun fact: Chris was known for his piercings and bandannas. He also does *South Park* impressions.

Joseph (Joey) Fatone
Born: 28 January 1977, Brooklyn, NYC
Fun fact: Joey was the eccentric in the band. He was famous for collecting *Superman* **memorabilia**.

James Lance (Lansten) Bass
Born: 4 May 1979, Clinton, Mississippi
Fun fact: Lance was fascinated by space travel. He wanted to pay for a trip into outer space.

Recording 'The star spangled banner' was popular back home in the USA.

Singing stars

The band's first recording was an **a cappella** version of 'The star spangled banner', the US national anthem.

'NSYNC: Chris, JC, Joey, Lance and Justin.

memorabilia valuable objects from an event, film, television programme or famous person's life

15

'NSYNC on tour

Touring with 'NSYNC was very **intensive**. The band made 300 appearances in two tours over just one year. They had to have notes backstage to remind them what city they were in that night!

Hitting the big time

At the beginning of 1998 'NSYNC were hardly known in the USA. The boys were selling millions of records across the rest of the world, though. All that changed with the release in the USA of their first single, 'I want you back', in the spring. Then their first album, 'NSYNC, was released a few months later.

Summer sales

The boys spent the first months of the year **promoting** their music. It was in the summer that sales really took off. In one week in August, more than a quarter of a million copies of the album sold in just five days! They also went on tour with Janet Jackson.

No Strings Attached

The early success of 'NSYNC was overshadowed by what they achieved with the album *No Strings Attached* in 2000. It broke all the records. It sold more than a million copies on the first day it was released, and nearly 2.5 million in the first week! Tickets to the band's 52-date US tour sold out on the first day that they went on sale. During the tour, the audience screamed so loudly that the boys had to wear earplugs!

Everywhere 'NSYNC went, thousands of fans were there to greet them.

Star words   intensive busy; demanding and challenging

'NYSNC spent long hours rehearsing to become a really exciting live band.

Devoted fans

The 'NSYNC tour in 1999 was very popular. The newspapers contained a story about fans who camped out in a skip for a week. They hoped that if they showed just what big fans they were they might win tickets to the New York concert!

'NSYNC takes off

'NSYNC were having a great time. They sang at the **Super Bowl**. They appeared on *The Simpsons*. Their website was the most popular music site in the world. In 1999 they won Best New Group at the American Music Awards.

The boys were not only popular with fans. They also won awards from the music industry.

Super Bowl final of the US National Football League championships

Going solo

★ ★ ★ ★ ★ ★ ★ ★ ★ ★

Wonderful music

Stevie Wonder played the harmonica section of 'Something like you', from the *Celebrity* album. Justin had to ask him to play it again as Stevie's harmonica was out of tune!

★ ★ ★ ★ ★ ★ ★ ★ ★ ★

'NYNSC's fourth album was called *Celebrity*. It was released in 2001 and sold nearly 2 million copies in the first week. This album was a turning point for Justin. He co-wrote seven of the songs, and co-produced five. Even on the recording of the previous album, *No Strings Attached*, he had started to take notice of what the **producers** did to create the album's sound. This was something that he got very interested in.

Taking control

On *Celebrity*, Justin began to take even more control. He arranged for his hero Stevie Wonder to play harmonica on one of the songs. Justin also asked Pharrell Williams and Chad Hugo, of the respected R 'n' B producers the Neptunes, to work on the album.

Album awards

The album received a **nomination** for a **Grammy** award for Best Pop Vocal Album. It was also nominated for the songs 'Gone' (2002) and 'Girlfriend' (2003).

Stevie Wonder lent his musical talents to *Celebrity*.

Star words

nomination put forward as one of the people to win an award

Going it alone gave Justin more freedom to make the music he wanted.

Leaving the band

There were rumours in newspapers and magazines that Justin was not happy in 'NSYNC and that the band was going to split. Justin never said that he wanted to leave, however. There was never an official break-up, but by 2002 he was writing a solo album.

'NSYNC alone

Justin was not the only one in 'NSYNC who wanted to do his own thing. Joey hoped to make it as an actor on Broadway. Chris Kirkpatrick has signed on to manage the Dallas band Ohno. JC has his own solo album, *Schizophrenic*.

★ ★ ★ ★ ★ ★ ★ ★ ★ ★ ★ ★

JC hopes to have his own solo success.

Grammy award given at the USA's most important annual popular music industry awards

7-Eleven

Justin wore a 7-Eleven cap in the video for 'Like I love you'. The store sold tens of thousands of the US$8 caps in just a few weeks because of the video.

Whole new sound

Justin released the solo single 'Like I love you' in October 2002. It was **produced** by the Neptunes, who had worked on 'NSYNC's last album. The song was a musical mix. It had Mexican **acoustic** guitars. It had hip-hop. It even featured a rap duo from Virginia called Clipse. It also had an amazing video. In it Justin showed off his dance moves. This reminded many people of early **break-dancing** moves. The single went to number two in the UK charts and number eleven in the USA.

> " It's definitely a new sound – not just from me, but period. I think it's cool. I hope everybody else does. "

Justin in the recording studio with the Neptunes.

Star words   acoustic non-electronic instruments; a non-electric guitar, for example

Justin chooses the best people to work with, like Timbaland (left) – shown here with rappers Missy Elliot and Flavor Flav.

★ ★ ★ ★ ★ ★ ★ ★ ★ ★ ★

Michael Jackson

Michael Jackson is one of Justin's musical heroes. His 1980s album, *Thriller*, still holds the world record for sales: more than 40 million. Justin says that Michael Jackson's music is an **inspiration** to him.

★ ★ ★ ★ ★ ★ ★ ★ ★ ★ ★

Michael Jackson's video for 'Thriller' was the first of its kind.

First hits

Justin's first solo single was followed by two more huge hits. The first was 'Cry me a river'. It was co-produced by the famous hip-hop producer Timbaland. It was a number three hit in the USA and reached number two in the UK. The song was another mix of styles: R 'n' B, hip-hop, slow rap, electronic horns and strings. Justin's dance moves were also making headlines, as well as his new **falsetto** singing style. The third single was co-written with the Neptunes. It was called 'Señorita' and was a mix of pop music, funk and **Latino** dance.

falsetto very high-pitched singing style
inspiration where you get your ideas from

All-star line-up

Justin's 'sound' has changed a lot since his days with 'NSYNC. This is because of the people he has worked with. As we have already seen, when he made *Celebrity*, Justin worked with Stevie Wonder and the Neptunes. He had toured with another hero, Janet Jackson, as early as 1998.

Collaborators

In 2002 Justin **collaborated** with musicians from the world of R 'n' B, hip-hop, dance and pop. He even appeared in an Elton John video in which he played Elton as a young man.

Childhood hero

Janet Jackson (above) was one of Justin's childhood heroes. She sings the backing vocals on Justin's track '(And she said) take me now'.

Justin and Nelly proved that two can sometimes be better than one.

Star words collaborate work together with another singer or musician on a song

Justin has worked with:

The Rolling Stones
Elton John
Lisa 'Left Eye' Lopes
Bubba Sparxxx
Nelly
Janet Jackson
Stevie Wonder
The Black Eyed Peas
Timbaland
The Neptunes

Justin has worked with world-famous musician Elton John.

The Black Eyed Peas.

Perhaps the most famous collaboration of all was with the rap star Nelly. Justin featured on the song 'Work it', from Nelly's *Welcome to Nellyville* album.

Learning

Just before Justin's solo album, *Justified*, came out, he talked about his experience working with so many different artists. 'It was so much fun, and I learned a lot about making music in a totally different way than I'm used to.'

Justin has been in showbiz since he was eleven years old. He has had a lot of success. There have been awards, record album sales and sell-out worldwide tours. There is the promise of many more in the future. So let's trace the highest points in Justin Timberlake's career – so far!

Justin won three awards at the 2003 MTV Europe Awards.

The highs

- First television show: Justin was a presenter on the *Mickey Mouse Club* from 1993 to 1995.
- Record sales: 'NSYNC sold millions of singles and albums. *No Strings Attached* sold 2.4 million copies in one week. That makes it the fastest selling album of all time!
- Going live: In 1999, 'NSYNC sold out on five **consecutive** nights at NYC's **prestigious** Radio City Music Hall.

Justin had a lot of success when he was part of 'NSYNC.

★ ★ ★ ★ ★ ★ ★ ★ ★ ★ ★

Awards

Justin's solo song, 'Like I love you' was nominated for Best Rap/Sung **collaboration** at the 2003 **Grammies**. Justin won the Best R 'n' B category at the British **MOBO** awards in the same year.

★ ★ ★ ★ ★ ★ ★ ★ ★

Star words   consecutive in a row or one after the other

They also sold out their 52-date US tour the same year in just 8 hours!

• Large scale: In July 2003 Justin appeared at a live concert with the Rolling Stones. This was a charity event in Toronto, Canada. Justin performed in front of a crowd of 470,000!

• Giving something back: In May 2000, the Justin Timberlake Foundation awarded its first musical grant to Justin's old school.

• Awards: Since he has gone solo, Justin has appeared at almost every big awards ceremony. He has received many **nominations**. He is also the perfect awards host. In 2003, for example, he co-hosted the MTV Movie Awards.

Justin on Justin

'I've had good and bad moments as a pop star. My best moment was performing in the half-time show at the **Super Bowl** [in 2001], in front of 200,000 people. My worst moment is when I fell off the stage in Cologne, Germany. We had a new spotlight operator that night and both Joey Fatone and I fell off into the pit. It was really embarrassing.'

Playing with the Rolling Stones saw Justin perform to one of his biggest audiences ever.

★ ★ ★ ★ ★ ★ ★ ★ ★ ★

Charity work

It is not only people in the music business who think a lot of Justin. The Justin Timberlake Foundation helps to improve music education in schools. He was praised for this by former US President Bill Clinton. He went to the White House and met the First Lady, Hillary Clinton.

prestigious of great value; highly regarded or thought of

Style and image

It is not just Justin's music that has changed since the early days with 'NSYNC. He has also changed his image. The young Justin was never happy with the way he looked. We have already mentioned that one of his childhood nicknames was 'brillo pad'. Justin says he once tried to cut all his hair off himself.

Standing out

As the lead singer of 'NSYNC, Justin was expected to stand out from the crowd. He was often made fun of for wearing string vests, baseball caps and flashy gold jewellery. When he tried something different it was not always successful. His **cornrow** hairstyle is just one example!

Stylish?

Justin was not the only member of 'NSYNC with style problems. There was Joey and his **goatee** and Superman t-shirts. Then there was Chris and his piercings and tattoos.

The Justin of today might wish the bandanna had covered his whole head!

Star words

cornrow hairstyle where the hair is arranged in tight, thin braids across the head

Justin's more
mature look.

★ ☆ ★ ☆ ★ ★ ☆ ★ ★ ★

Eligible

In 1999, *People* magazine voted Justin the Most Beautiful Person of the Year. Britney Spears came second. Three years later, the same magazine named Justin America's Most **Eligible Bachelor** of the Year.

★ ☆ ★ ☆ ★ ★ ★ ★ ★ ★

Justin looks smart and stylish in a suit.

Growing up

Some people have also criticized Justin for copying Michael Jackson's look with a **fedora** hat and white gloves. His image has improved a lot, though. In his videos he has a more adult, urban and hip-hop image. He has cropped his hair short. He is now often seen wearing fashionable suits from designer labels.

fedora old-fashioned type of hat made of soft felt, with a curled brim

Trickster

Many of Justin's fans may have spoken to him without knowing it. For a while his mobile phone number was almost the same as the number for a leading pizza chain. Justin often used to get orders for deliveries. Sometimes he played jokes on the callers, taking the orders before telling them they had the wrong number.

The Flaming Lips are some of music's more quirky dressers.

Justin has sold millions of records. He is often voted the most stylish or the sexiest man on the planet. These are not the only reasons why he is so popular, though. He also has a lot of charm and a good sense of humour. Many of his videos show this. The cheeky video for his **collaboration** with Nelly, 'Work it', is one example. He has also appeared on British television with one of his favourite bands, The Flaming Lips, dressed in a furry animal costume!

Entertainer

Justin is a great entertainer. It is no wonder that **veteran** pop stars like The Rolling Stones asked him to play at their charity concert in Canada, or that Elton John wanted Justin to play him in a music video. Justin has even become the face and sound of an international fast-food chain.

28

Star words

spokesperson someone who represents a person or a company

Keeping grounded

Justin knows how to keep his feet on the ground. Justin thanks his oldest and best childhood friend, Trace Ayala, for stopping him from being big-headed. Justin says: 'He makes me feel like I'm on Earth – he's unfazed by all this craziness.'

For his live performances Justin always gives his fans something different.

Star fact

In 2003 Justin was asked to perform for the Queen. A **spokesperson** for Buckingham Palace commented: 'It just goes to show that no woman on Earth is immune to his charms!'

Sister act

Justin has a sense of humour and never seems to lose his cool. In November 2002 he appeared on the Nickelodeon chat show *All That*. Britney Spears's little sister, Jamie Lynn (above), came on dressed as an 84-year-old bouncer. She catches Justin trying to sneak into a club. She pulls down his trousers to reveal multi-coloured underwear.

Personal interests

Justin's favourites

Colour: baby blue

Food: pasta, cereal and pepperoni pizza

Accessory: sunglasses

Film stars: Brad Pitt, Samuel L Jackson, Meg Ryan

'NSYNC song: 'God must have spent a little more time on u'

Television programme: Seinfeld

Film: Ferris Bueller's Day Off

Justin's first passion is music. When he was in 'NSYNC he called his band mates his 'second family'. Since he has gone solo he has improved his piano and guitar skills. He has worked to improve his dance moves. He has also learned from his **producer** friends such as Timbaland and the Neptunes.

Remember your roots

Justin knows how lucky he has been. He has never forgotten where he comes from or the people who helped him be successful. In an interview with the *New York Post* in December 2000 he said: 'I remember my parents always saying, "Remember your roots. Whatever happens, remember your roots, remember where you came from."'

Justin is a talented keyboard player as well as a singer.

Star words   fortunate lucky

Giving something back

Justin wants to help people who are less **fortunate** than he is. He set up the Justin Timberlake Foundation in 1999. This is a programme that gives money for music and arts education in schools. In May 2000 the Foundation awarded its first grant to Justin's old elementary school.

New projects

Since he has changed his own image, Justin has been thinking about setting up his own clothes and accessories range. He has also opened his own restaurant in Los Angeles. It is called Chi and is inside the Hyatt Hotel on Sunset Boulevard.

★ ★ ★ ★ ★ ★ ★ ★ ★ ★ ★ ★

Basketball

Justin is a keen basketball player and often plays in matches for charity.

★ ★ ★ ★ ★ ★ ★ ★ ★ ★

Justin showed off his new dance moves at this UK concert in December 2003.

Justin loves his Harleys.

Work hard, play hard

Justin is a **dedicated** professional, but he still tries to find time to relax. He spends long days touring, recording and receiving awards. He needs his time off, too.

Basketball magic

After music, Justin's biggest passion is probably basketball. He is a huge fan of the basketball legend Michael Jordan, who retired in 2003. Justin's favourite basketball team is the Orlando Magic team.

Cars and bikes

Justin loves cars, and has a Mercedes M Class, a BMW roadster, a Dodge Viper and a Cadillac Escalade. He also has a passion for motorbikes. He gave Harley Davidsons to his mother and stepfather as presents. They were not the only bikes in the household. Justin says: 'We have about seven now.'

Justin is a big fan of Michael Jordan.

Star words   dedicated hard-working

Throughout his childhood Justin collected basketball **memorabilia**. He is a good basketball player, too. His elementary school was impressed by his performances. After he left, they kept his number 12 shirt and did not let anyone else wear that number.

Justin at home

Justin now has his own house in the Hollywood Hills, but his Memphis home will always be the family home. There are **plasma screens** and video game consoles in almost every room. There is also a pinball game.

On course

Justin can sometimes be spotted playing golf, one of his new-found interests. His US$8million house in the Hollywood Hills is designed in a Mexican style. It stands in 10 acres of land and has a tennis court.

Justin on TV

Although music is his first job, Justin is also interested in acting. He made a guest appearance on *Sabrina the Teenage Witch* in 1996. He also appeared in the US television film *Model Behaviour* in 2000. There are lots of rumours that Justin will appear in feature films. He has not denied them all!

Golf is a relaxing escape from Justin's hectic life.

plasma screen modern flat screen often used for laptop computer screens and large-screen televisions

Media spotlight

Beyoncé is another solo success. She won five **Grammy** awards in 2004.

Solo success

Justin is not the first singer to become even more famous after going solo. Beyoncé Knowles was already a huge star with Destiny's Child. Since she released her own solo album, she has become even more successful.

Justin has never been camera shy. He often admits that he feels most comfortable when he has an audience. Before he appeared in the *Mickey Mouse Club* on television, he had tried out at every music **audition** he could get to. You may remember that he sang in a boy band at his elementary school. Justin loves the camera, and the camera also loves him.

Fan favourite

When Justin joined 'NSYNC he was the junior member of the band. He was only fourteen years old. Some of his band mates were much older and more experienced. By 1999 Justin had become the favourite with the fans as well as the press. Justin never meant to attract more attention than the other boys, but in every 'NSYNC interview, half of the questions were for him alone.

★ Star fact

When he was with 'NSYNC, Justin and his band mates made a **cameo** appearance on the cartoon show *The Simpsons*.

Famous girlfriend

From 2000 to 2002, Justin and his equally famous girlfriend were one of pop's most glamorous couples. His relationship with Britney Spears made Justin even more popular with the **media**. During those years, though, it was Britney who was the centre of attention. She was much more famous than Justin.

Star words

cameo short appearance in a television programme, video or film

In the spotlight

Now Justin has become the 'most **eligible bachelor** in the world'. He has a best-selling album and singles. He has award-winning videos. He has had film offers. His face is on magazine covers. He has a new style of music and a new fashion look. He is now much more famous than the other 'NSYNC members. He gets the sort of **publicity** that Britney does.

Justin is always an impressive live performer.

Joker

Justin once appeared on the MTV hidden camera show *Punk'd*. He played a joke on rock singer Kelly Osbourne (below). He arranged for record executives to have a meeting with the rock star. They told Kelly that she had to change her image to look more like Christina Aguilera or Britney Spears!

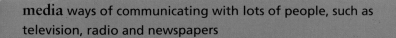

media ways of communicating with lots of people, such as television, radio and newspapers

Engaged?

In July 2000 a UK newspaper (The *News of the World*) claimed that Justin had proposed to Britney. Apparently he put a £30,000 engagement ring on her finger while they were sipping coffee in a cafe. This, however, was never confirmed!

Celebrity teamwork

Britney Spears is a name often **associated** with Justin. They met when they were both new **Mouseketeers** on the *Mickey Mouse Club*. They became friends. They played table tennis in between shooting for the programme.

Early friendship

After the *MMC* series ended in 1995, Britney went to New York. Justin returned to Memphis and went back to school.

★ Star fact

While 'NSYNC was becoming the biggest boy band in the world, Britney made it huge. Her single, 'Baby one more time' was a big hit in 1998. Her album of the same name sold more than 20 million copies.

Britney and the 'NYSNC boys toured together in the early days.

Star words   associated to do with or mentioned along with

Justin and Britney finally admitted that they were an item.

It was only after he had joined the band 'NSYNC that he began to see Britney again. She had started her own music career. She even supported the boys on tour.

Going public

Justin and Britney were old friends. They often went to **premieres** and music awards together. Soon the rumours started that they were an item. At first the couple denied they were more than just friends. Then Britney cracked under the pressure. In an interview with the music magazine *Rolling Stone* in May 2000, she admitted that she and Justin had kissed. When she realized what she had done she laughed and said: 'Oh my gosh, my manager is going to kill me.' Finally they had 'gone public'.

Young love

Justin and Britney seemed like the perfect couple. Their families were happy about the relationship. Although it took them years actually to go out, it looked as if it had been love at first sight. When Justin was just twelve, he told his grandmother, Sadie, that he thought he would marry Britney one day.

premiere first showing of a film, often with celebrities invited

Celebrity couples

Some famous couples do stay together, but many cannot survive the **media** attention. Look at all the problems that Jennifer Lopez and Ben Affleck had when they were engaged. Couples often say that it is hard to stay together when their jobs mean that they are apart for most of the time.

Double trouble

Justin and Britney seemed to be the 'dream' couple of the pop world. Wherever they went together, pictures of them appeared in newspapers and magazines. There were problems for them, though. Britney and Justin were often on tour in distant parts of the world. They would often work long hours. This meant they could not spend much time together.

Splitting up

It started to appear that Justin and Britney were not happy. At the **premiere** of her movie, *Crossroads*, in March 2002, Britney said that she was 'not in an **intense** relationship with anyone'. There were even rumours that she had started going out with someone else. No one apart from Britney and Justin really knows what happened, but it became clear that they were no longer a couple.

Jennifer Lopez and Ben Affleck had lots of problems with the media.

★ Star fact

Justin had a 'pet name' for Britney – 'Pinky'. He calls her 'Pinky' on the **sleevenotes** to the 'NSYNC album *Celebrity*. This is because of the ring she wears on her little finger, or 'pinky'. Britney called Justin 'stinky'! No explanation needed!

Star words

sleevenotes notes inside an album cover. Performers use them to thank all the people who have helped them.

What went wrong?

Justin refused to say exactly what went wrong between him and Britney. In an interview with the UK magazine *Marie Claire* in May 2003 he said: 'No one knows what went on between Britney and me except us. [...] We're friends now. We're not mad at each other.'

The cameras followed Justin and Britney everywhere.

Alyssa Milano was one of the women seen out with Justin after Britney.

Single again

Justin might have gone solo in 2002, but that does not mean he was alone. There seemed to be a lot of girls who wanted to go out with him. He was seen out with the actress Alyssa Milano. He was also seen with Janet Jackson and 'NSYNC dancer Jenna Dewan.

intense very emotional

Big seller

Justified sold more than 3 million copies by the end of 2003. It also earned Justin respect from within the music industry. His mum said in an interview with *Rolling Stone* magazine in December 2003: 'At the VMAs, when he won the award [for Best Male Video] and Eminem and 50 Cent stood up to applaud, that left such an impression on him.'

By the spring of 2002, Justin was single again. It also looked as if he might be going solo as a musician. He and the other 'NSYNC boys went to the Cannes film festival that year. They talked about their plans for a joint film project. By that time, Justin was already preparing to record a solo album. Then he had an accident while rehearsing for a show in Toronto. He broke a bone in his foot. The accident gave Justin a chance to take some time off. He returned to his family home in Memphis to get better and have some time to himself.

Even in that tracksuit, there is no way Justin is going to escape the press!

Star words

media glare attention of newspapers, magazines and television

Taking a break

The accident delayed Justin's solo projects, but it also gave him time to rest and decide what he wanted to do with his life. What he wanted to do was to work on his new material and new sound.

First singles

By the end of the summer Justin was very much back in the **media glare**. His first two singles, 'Like I love you' and 'Cry me a river' were hits across the world. His album *Justified* made him one of the hottest solo artists in the world.

Justin out with his mum.

Justin's mum

Justin and his mum often go out together. Justin has admitted that she often comes home later at night than he does! In an interview with the *Herald* newspaper, Justin explained: 'We have a very special relationship. She's always been there beside me.'

Justin and Chris Kirkpatrick show the press that the 'NSYNC 'family' have never fallen out.

Now and then

★ ★ ★ ★ ★ ★ ★ ★ ★ ★

Music

What will Justin's music be like in the future? Justin's friend and producer Timbaland made a **prediction** as early as 2002: 'He's about to become so much more famous than he already is that it's going to blow people away. The stuff he's doing is so cool and revolutionary.'

★ ★ ★ ★ ★ ★ ★ ★ ★ ★

Justin has been on front covers of fashion, style and music magazines from all around the world. He has been the lead singer in the fastest-selling band of all time. He was one half of one of the biggest celebrity couples on the planet. Now he is a huge solo star. He has written for and **collaborated** with the biggest stars in the music business. So what now for Justin?

Hot property

A couple of months after the release of *Justified*, Justin said: 'I think this album has established my identity. I think this was my coming-out party.' Justin is certainly hot property now. Many of the world's top artists have asked to work with him. He has worked with the chart-topping hip-hop group The Black Eyed Peas. He has won some of the top music awards in the world.

Not just music

Justin is not only making music. He has signed a contract as a television **sports correspondent** to talk about basketball, his favourite sport. He has also opened his own restaurant. That is a busy schedule!

Justin in the video for 'I'm lovin' it'.

On screen

Justin may be appearing on screen. He was sent a script to play the role of Jimmy Olsen in the next *Superman* film.

Star words **prediction** what someone thinks might happen in the future

He has said he would like to be in a film version of the musical *Rent*. Whatever Justin does next, one thing is clear – he is set to become an even bigger star than he is now.

Being solo does not mean you cannot be a team player, as Justin showed with The Black Eyed Peas.

Justin and Cameron Diaz trying to avoid the attention of the cameras.

Love

After the split with Britney, Justin claimed that he needed a break. That has not stopped the rumours. He has been linked with models, actresses and singers. The only person he has admitted to going out with is the Hollywood star Cameron Diaz.

sports correspondent someone who comments on sports on television, radio or in newspapers

Find out more

Books
Justin Timberlake: The Unofficial Book,
  Martin Roach (Virgin Books, 2003)
Justin Timberlake: Unauthorized, Michael
  Heatley (Contender Books, 2003)
'NSYNC with Justin, Matt Netter
  (Simon Pulse, 1999)
Pop People: Justin, Michael-Anne Johns
  (Scholastic, 2000)

Audiobook (CD)
Maximum Justin Timberlake (2003)

DVD/VHS
Live from London (2003)
Justified (2003)
Startrax: Justin Timberlake/'NSYNC (2003)
'NSYNC – Popodyssey (2001)
'NSYNC: Making the Tour (2000)
*'NSYNC: Live From Madison Square
  Gardens* (2000)

Discography
Albums
Justified (2002)

Singles
'Work it' (Nelly and Justin Timberlake)
  (2003)
'Rock your body' (2003)
'Señorita' (2003)

'Cry me a river' (2002)
'Like I love you' (2002)

Albums with 'NSYNC
Celebrity (2001)
No Strings Attached (2000)
The Winter Album (1998)
'NSYNC (1998)

Websites
Justin's official website is:
http://www.justintimberlake.com
The Internet is full of news about what Justin
is up to. A good search engine is:
http://www.yahooligans.com
A good website for music news is:
http://www.bbc.co.uk/totp
Justin also features regularly on celebrity
news websites. Try this one:
http://www.eonline.com

Disclaimer
All the Internet addresses (URLs) given in this book were valid at the
time of going to press. However, due to the dynamic nature of the
Internet, some addresses may have changed, or sites may have ceased to
exist since publication. While the author, packager and publishers regret
any inconvenience this may cause readers, no responsibility for any such
changes can be accepted by either the author, packager or the publishers.

Glossary

a cappella music in which no instruments, just singing voices, are used

acoustic non-electronic instruments; a non-electric guitar, for example

associated to do with or mentioned along with

audition interview for a musician or actor, where they show their skills

bluegrass mixture of country music and blues that is common in the southern and midwest states of the USA

break-dancing energetic form of street dancing popular in the 1980s. Break-dancers would often compete against each other to see whose moves were the best.

cameo short appearance in a television programme, video or film

casting director person who picks out new talent to appear on television or in films

choreographer person who makes up dance routines for pop videos and live performances

collaborate work together with another singer or musician on a song

consecutive in a row or one after the other

cornrow hairstyle where the hair is arranged in tight, thin braids across the head

cover version recording or a performance of a song by a different performer from the original

dedicated hard-working

demo examples of songs recorded by musicians who are just starting out. They often send demos to record producers to try and get noticed.

eligible bachelor single man who is popular with women

falsetto very high-pitched singing style

fedora old-fashioned type of hat made of soft felt, with a curled brim

fortunate lucky

gig live performance

goatee beard that covers the chin and moustache area, leaving the neck and cheeks bare

Grammy award given at the USA's most important annual popular music industry awards

icon important or famous person that you look up to and try to be like

inspiration where you get your ideas from

intense very emotional

intensive busy; demanding and challenging

Latino from Latin America. Popular music styles include salsa, mambo and son Cubano.

media ways of communicating with lots of people, such as television, radio and newspapers

media glare attention of newspapers, magazines and television

memorabilia valuable objects from an event, film, television programme or famous person's life

Mouseketeers name given to the young stars of the *Mickey Mouse Club*

nomination put forward as one of the people to win an award

plasma screen modern flat screen often used for laptop computer screens and large-screen televisions

prediction what someone thinks might happen in the future

premiere first showing of a film, often with celebrities invited

prestigious of great value; highly regarded or thought of

producer person in charge of making a record, film or television show

production arranging and mixing the music when recording a song

promote tell people about a new product

publicity attention from the media

sleevenotes notes inside an album cover. Performers use them to thank all the people who have helped them.

spokesperson someone who represents a person or a company

sports correspondent someone who comments on sports on television, radio or in newspapers

suburb outskirts of a city where people live

Super Bowl final of the US National Football League championships

trademark something that is typical about a person

tribute band musical group that plays another band's songs in a very similar style

veteran someone with a lot of experience in something

Index

50 Cent 40

Affleck, Ben 38
Aguilera, Christina 11, 35
Ayala, Trace 29

Backstreet Boys 12–14
Bass, Lance 13–15
Black Eyed Peas 23, 42–43
Buckingham Palace 29

Chasez, Joshua (JC) 10, 12, 14–15, 19
Clinton, Bill 25
Clinton, Hillary 25
Clipse 20

Destiny's Child 34
Dewan, Jenna 39
Diaz, Cameron 43

Eminem 40

Fatone, Joey 12, 15, 19, 25–26
Fisher, Carrie 15
Flaming Lips, The 28

Grammy Awards 18, 24, 34

Harless, Paul 6–7
Hart, Melissa Joan 10
Hugo, Chad 18

Jackson, Janet 16, 22–23, 39
Jackson, Michael 13, 21, 27

Jackson, Samuel L. 30
John, Elton 22–23, 28
Jordan, Michael 32
Justin Timberlake Foundation 4, 25, 31

Kirkpatrick, Chris 12, 14–15, 19, 26, 41
Knowles, Beyoncé 34

Lewis, Jerry Lee 7
Lopes, Lisa 'Left Eye' 23
Lopez, Jennifer 38

Milano, Alyssa 39
MOBO Awards 24
Mouseketeers 10, 12, 36

Nelly 22–23, 28
Neptunes, The 18, 20, 22–23, 30
New Kids on the Block 8–9, 13
'NSYNC 4–5, 12–20, 14, 16, 18, 22–24, 26, 30, 34–40, 38, 40–42

Osbourne, Kelly 35

Pearlman, Lou 14
Pitt, Brad 30
Presley, Elvis 7

Robson, Wade J. 12
Rolling Stones 23, 25, 28
Ryan, Meg 30

Sparxx, Bubba 23
Spears, Britney 8, 11, 27, 29, 34–39, 43

Spears, Jamie Lynn 29
Super Bowl 17, 25

Timbaland 21, 23, 30, 42
Timberlake, Justin
albums 16, 18, 22–24, 38, 40–42
awards 17–18, 24–25, 32, 35, 37, 40, 42
charities 4, 25, 31
collaborations 22–23, 28, 42
early life 4, 6–11, 8, 33–34
family 6–7, 30, 41
films 40, 42–43
future 5, 42–43
image 26–29, 31
interests 30–33, 42
'NSYNC 4–5, 12–20, 22, 24, 30, 34, 37–40
singles 14, 16, 20, 23
'Cry me a river' 21, 41
'Like I love you' 21, 41
'Señorita' 21
television 29, 33, 42
Mickey Mouse Club (MMC) 8–12, 24, 34, 36

Westbrook, Bob 8, 12
Williams, Pharrell 18
Wonder, Stevie 13, 18, 22–23
Wright, Johnny 14
Wylie, Pete 12

Titles in the *Star Files* series include:

Hardback   1 844 43829 5

Hardback   1 844 43830 9

Hardback   1 844 43833 3

Hardback   1 844 43834 1

Hardback   1 844 43831 7

Hardback   1 844 43832 5

Find out about the other titles in this series on our website www.raintreepublishers.co.uk